Series by Stephen Kagarise

Hysterion: Surrealist Love Poems

Zombie Chronicles

The Diary of Madame Rentz

Cyberpunk 1876

Approved Jawbone

COMPENDIUM OF RIVALS

COMPENDIUM OF RIVALS

Stephen Kagarise

Hysterion Press

ISBN : 979-8-9992019-3-5

"Love has its own dark morality when rivalry enters in."

— Sue Bridehead

CONTENTS

Strife's Dark Minions

That there is the scowl of opposition
is known and expected, for what that is
lovely has ever escaped such noiseless
action, replete with all the other games
called together to advance wealth or power?
Ambitious dogs in quest of adventure
sustain themselves in this glorious work
with the sublime energy of women's
endurance, and in no instance was there
a speech made whispering resignation.

Beauty Is No Cheap Humbug

The genuine, original and pure
article thus gives them a parting kick.
Poets sing it, romancers furnish it
in abundance, for all the world worships
tall, queenly beauties. Civilization
is as pretty does, where the balance is
largely with delight in loving, in lots
to suit the beaming countenance of men.

Boiled Lobster This Season

She had a strong lobby present, her gloves
by the kid, her furs by the seal, her dress
by the silkworm, her whalebones by the whale.
Even the color of her cheek, making
old clothes look like new, is supplied by the
insect cochineal. That jolly pow-wow
staring him in the face could give offense,
saying they would take by force what don't belong
to them, plainly visible on breaking open.

Debris of a Blast Blown Out

He always refused, saying in a tone
of pleasantry, "Go your way, poor children."
We must go on hoping, with but little
to expect, however, in the sweet by
and by. That grand army who incurred his
displeasure deny the reports, and say
that some men's bodies are no straighter than
their minds, unsparing in epigrammatic
comments evasive of the main question.

Doctrine of Perfectionism

Their physical and mental endurance
is something wonderful. Close, active, sharp,
with a thoroughness heretofore unknown
they search every nook and corner, standing
upon each other's shoulders. Before this,
they had smiled at songs, dances, the farce
of renewed courtship dearer than wrecked goods
at auction. Shrinkage of hard times began
to consume at one end the vexed question.

So Much Past the Starting Point

However they may call, and however sharp
they may be in questioning, no one can
tell what he means to do, doubtful whether
this agent of the oyster trade will join in
play a few brief weeks, the beasts astray on
the prairies. It is the upward pull that cuts
for want of care. He declined to express
his views, and the hands are stationary while
with us the face of the clock always moves.

Read It from His Smiling Face

If anyone chooses to quarrel with him
about it, I have no objection. His mother
saw an accomplished man and a gallant
officer, as regular in his habits as clock-
work. The blinds were down at the window
of his shop, based upon the fate of those
who had gone before. One for ingress, one
for egress. The school-book question is
not a terror to anybody now quite at home.

First Noted in the Plain of Shinar

Lottie and Belle have plied their vocation
with inventive genius, prepared to do
all kinds of jobbing when you are looking
for a place to amuse yourself. Drop in
and display fine taste in liquors and cigars.
The method proposed is by hydraulic
pressure, with nozzles long enough to go
from headquarters down to the point where
complaint originates those land pirates.

Leading Men Making Mistakes

"My name is Beauty and I belong to
an ill-tempered joke." Such was engraved on
the collar of a canine seen frolicking
about, putting as much style in his new
and gaudy colors as a French dancing
master. Fractious animals put so much
to idle purposes. Nothing can restrain
horse flesh in sausages, without injuring
fat ducks sitting upon the pearly edge.

It Is Well Enough to Be Discrete

Was there ever a despotism more
relentless and cruel? The desire, as
expressed in many letters, was to get
away to some place where the storms are
wiped out with a sympathizing tear.
More rain yesterday, but prospects of fair
weather soon command a fabulous price.
We intend to hew a fortune out of fertile
valleys, creating such a need that he
thinks would profit by the investment.

Thoroughly Artistic and Satisfying

A full-length portrait of Martha living
here on these faraway plains needs no praise
from us. All the renegades in the country
have gone heavily for it, and doubtless
there will be a good chance for bargains.
They have plenty to do, riding over its
careful study of hands, bestowed on them
as best suits their inclination. The month
of time spent on this picture thinks so too.
The effect of the whole shows technique
in rude contours having something to say.

Privy Councils Settle the Matter

The question, Camille, is not how
cheaply we can manage to keep body
and soul together, but how we can
bring acquiescence to the inevitable.
To live is something more than making
a piratical raid on fishermen along
the river. All pinching and restricting
of diet kick the beam intent only on
stopping outgo, and perpetually obtrude
upon public notice salting work that
spends something for a bath in "ropy"
tapioca soup, as dry as the Dead Sea.

An Expert in the Bare Necessities

We look at the postman afar off, with
eager eyes, and watch his approaching footstep
with new interest. He comes and goes,
but he leaves nothing behind. Tedium
and monotony reign. It is like the coming
of the end. The mountain of exchanges
has melted and gone, and nothing now stands
in its place. Something must be done, rain
or shine, snow or frost. It must be made out
of nothing, in the absence of something,
and in exactly that ratio for fractions under
a diamond ring. Three or four days can be
tided over, but a week or a month is neither
instructive nor entertaining. The custom is
still everywhere the gadfly and the phoenix.
Take the right side of practice, particularly
on frequented walks, in which some become
investors caused by the crowding together.

Lovingly Riding Toward a Crisis

As fair as any petted belle, she
stood raining hard and well-directed blows
upon the stubborn iron, and the lovely
tinge of pink and red spread over face
and neck. Her sleeves were rolled up to
her elbow, and loose blouse coat gave
evidence of robust health, quietly at work.
A bit of aniseed cake that he sought for
he ate approvingly, but on another occasion
spit it out without observation. Though
twenty years his senior, she married him.
The good news is being spread widely
among the fraternity, who came to her door
during their brief honeymoon, mingling
tears and kisses in that vast desert expanse.

Rainbow Spans the Vaulted Dome

The almost superhuman exertions
putting this and that together wonder
when if ever the day long hoped for
will come. Shall the devotees quit their
incendiary business, retired to rest
at an early hour, drawing the curtains
so calm, so serene, so joyous as to
inspire the blooming morn to get up
for shame? See how Aurora throws her
fresh-quilted colors through the air,
sweet slugabed, the dew bespangling.

Wasting His Time in Idle Regrets

Many an assassin's knife and pistol
lurked in curious deep holes, ready soon
as a riot came. Apparently seeking
a fight, their stomachs contained human
flesh, bones, and particles of clothing.
Things that showed plainly the fate of poor
Downing, a young English mechanic,
by one star and another star forced to run
through narrow gorges. The observer
can see the change in an hour's watch.

Prime Mover in Such a Reception

Many moves now being made upon
the grand chessboard are not explainable,
but it is nevertheless true that work
has begun, pending negotiations to be
determined hereafter. The projectors
mean business, ready like vultures to prey
on a fine social gentleman, in the line
for recognition. And the entire company
can be found on foot, on horseback, in
wagons, surveying complaints when all
other medicines have failed. Our Bismarck
has ordered his lady to bathe in the bath
provided by nature, and again she floats.

Without Making Others Suspicious

See what druggists say about pain in
the back, side and loin. He made it a study,
and its cause, he says, is awakening
after a lethargic sleep of nearly seven
years. He made his mark among the
"society ladies," teaching penmanship
to any who wish to avail themselves
of the opportunity, plowing through the
mud daily between a pair of chromos.
Nothing more agreeably surprises us than
to observe the transit of Venus, a route
we travel over rather than have it lie idle.

The Most Captivating Novelette

Here you are, plunged into this monster
mass meeting, with all sorts of creeping
things and slimy creatures, resolved to live
and to die. The question is, how will you
come out of it? An outlet is desirable, is in
fact a necessity, and we should like very
much to see the plan proposed worked up.
But such was not her destiny, and with
due regard for a pure love story, its price
is but fifty cents, "all too short" in spite
of the thrilling incidents, rippling dancing.

Kind Wishes for His Future Welfare

Some were attempting what is either
silly, vicious or impossible, and others of
the worst tramped it along these lines
through the tides and currents, sands and shoals
upon which the light of civilization has
never shed its redeeming light. Therefore
he would go to Peru, a place where he
was yearning for rest, peace and quietness.
It is enough to make a man kick a dog.
Still they come, the boss of the town,
a compound extract of extraordinary silk
parasols. And if the machine cannot be
made to work, send that umbrella home.

All Taken with This Sense of Duty

We fought a long war after the terrible
sacrifices made. But we are compelled to
do so, for the pleasure of the act. Gaze
in admiration and be happy, as in the days
of "lang syne," and see the pantomime
fixing and mixing. Green, luxuriant grass,
beautiful flowers, and the warbling of
a thousand robins all combined to make
this a modern Eden. Humpty Dumpty does
not once allude to distress in cashmere.

—An impromptu mock auction sale of women was amusing and profitable at first in a Racine, Wisconsin, church fair. The young men bid liberally for the attractive girls, and it was all very funny indeed until an ugly but influential sister was put up. The autioneer was compelled to knock her down at 25 cents, and she was so angry that she put on her things and went home.

The Daily Astorian, May 6, 1879

SPECIAL THANKS TO

D. C. Ireland, Publisher of *The Daily Astorian*

and the University of Oregon Libraries

COVER ART

Massimo Buon Mercato

by Leonetto Cappiello